# Healing Warrior

## A Story about
## Sister Elizabeth Kenny

by Emily Crofford
illustrations by Steve Michaels

A Carolrhoda Creative Minds Book

Carolrhoda Books, Inc./Minneapolis

*To Robert P., number one beloved*

The author would like to especially thank Margaret Opdahl Ernest and Betty Henry.

This book was made possible in part by a grant provided to the author by the Minnesota State Arts Board through an appropriation by the Minnesota Legislature, and in part by a grant from the National Endowment for the Arts.

LIBRARY OF CONGRESS CATALOGING-IN-PUBLICATION DATA

Crofford, Emily.
   Healing warrior : a story about Sister Elizabeth Kenny / by Emily Crofford : illustrations by Steve Michaels.
      p.      cm. — (A Carolrhoda creative minds book)
   Summary: A biography of the Australian nurse who developed a successful method of treating and rehabilitating polio patients and persisted in the struggle, despite ridicule and opposition, to have her methods accepted.
   ISBN 0-87614-382-6
   1. Kenny, Elizabeth—Juvenile literature. 2. Nurses—Australia—Biography—Juvenile literature. 3. Poliomyelitis—Patients—Rehabilitation—History—Juvenile literature. [1. Kenny, Elizabeth. 2. Nurses. 3. Poliomyelitis—Patients—Rehabilitation—History.]
   I. Michaels, Steve, ill. II. Title. III. Series.
RT37.K39C76   1989
362.1'96835'0092—dc20
[B]                                                       89-33474
[92]                                                         CIP
                                                              AC

Manufactured in the United States of America

   2   3   4   5   6   7   8   9   10   99   98   97   96   95   94   93   92   91   90

# Table of Contents

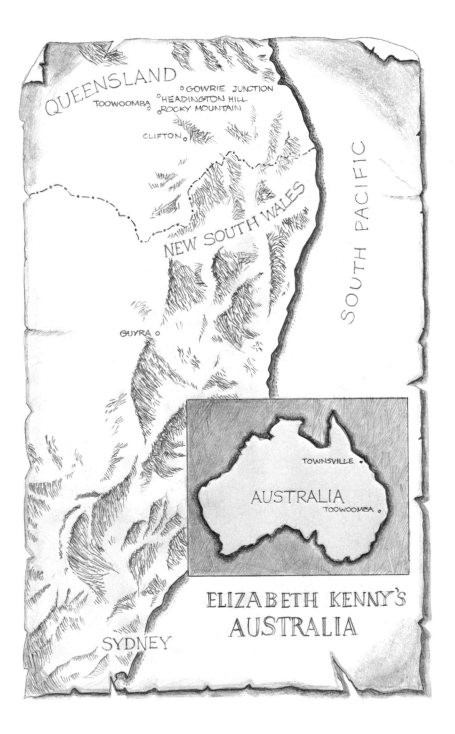

QUEENSLAND

TOOWOOMBA ○ GOWRIE JUNCTION
○ HEADINGTON HILL
○ ROCKY MOUNTAIN

CLIFTON ○

NEW SOUTH WALES

GUYRA ○

SOUTH PACIFIC

TOWNSVILLE ·

AUSTRALIA

TOOWOOMBA ·

SYDNEY

ELIZABETH KENNY'S
AUSTRALIA

# Chapter One

On a cold morning in 1888, Elizabeth Kenny dressed for her first day of school. She put on black stockings and high-button shoes, woolen drawers, a petticoat, a long dress, and a white pinafore. She looked at herself in the mirror, then picked up her wrap and waited for her sister Julia.

Although she was eight years old, Elizabeth had never been to school. Her family had moved around a lot in New South Wales, Australia. In some places they had lived, there hadn't been a school. At their new homestead in Guyra, there was a school only two miles away.

Elizabeth was a little nervous about going to school, but her mother assured her that she had nothing to worry about. "You've learned a lot at our home lessons," Mrs. Kenny said. After evening chores, Elizabeth's father taught arithmetic and

Latin. Her mother read from the Bible and quoted Shakespeare, Sir Walter Scott, and Goethe.

Rachel, the oldest, and Henry, the next-to-oldest, didn't go to school. They stayed at home to help with the work on the farm. The twins, Mary and Margaret, weren't old enough to go to school. And Elizabeth's little brother, Willie, was just a baby.

Every morning, Elizabeth and Julia met their cousins. They walked together to the one-room school. While they read and recited, Elizabeth was careful not to break any of the rules. Pupils who did "got the cane." Everyone was afraid of the teacher's cane.

On the way home, Elizabeth sometimes told stories about things that had happened in other places where the Kennys had lived. Her cousins laughed and said, "Oh, what tarradiddles you tell." That meant she had made up parts of the stories to make them exciting.

At home, there were always chores—cooking and dishwashing, sewing and ironing. Elizabeth didn't like housework. She preferred to help her father. On horseback, she rounded up the cows that had been let out to graze and brought them back to the barn for milking. As long as she could be outside, Elizabeth didn't even mind weeding and helping to harvest the potatoes.

After the cold Australian winter months of July and August, she particularly liked being out of doors when spring arrived. Buttercups and bluebells, tiny pink traveler's joy, and sweet-scented clover carpeted the meadows. Grasses and shrubs and trees grew in the wild, uncultivated land called "the bush."

Elizabeth often took a book into the bush with her. She would find a comfortable rock to sit on and read for hours. When she tired of reading, she daydreamed. One of her daydreams was that like Grandfather Moore, a former sea captain, she would someday go to America.

Kangaroos hopped by and koala bears munching on eucalyptus leaves peered down at her. Sometimes she saw a goanna, a lizard that looked like a dragon when it grew to its full six-foot length. It would eat chickens and eggs, but Elizabeth knew it was harmless to people.

Some of the animals, though, were very dangerous. Once, when Elizabeth was exploring the bush, a death adder blocked her path. In those days there was no antidote to its venom, and victims of the viper's bite would die within minutes.

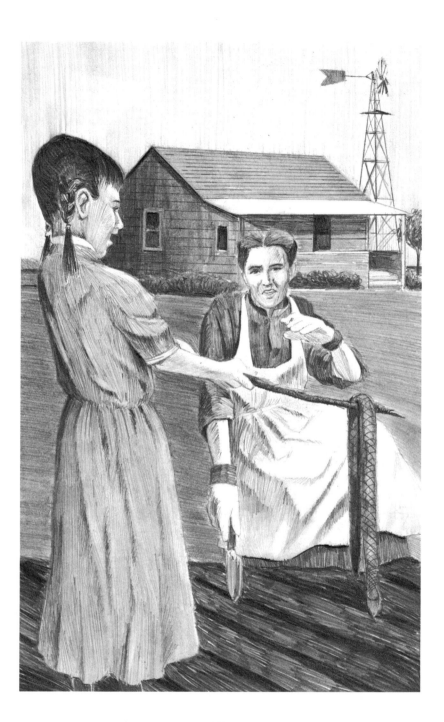

Although Elizabeth knew this, she grabbed a stick and pounded the snake. It finally stopped wriggling and lay still. She slid the stick under the limp snake and picked it up. With the snake dangling off the stick in front of her, she proudly went home to show her mother, who was working in the garden.

"We don't have to worry about this one anymore," Elizabeth said. She put the end of the stick on the ground to let the "dead" adder slide off. It promptly slithered away.

Many of Elizabeth's relatives also lived in Guyra. Her favorite game was racing on horseback with her cousin Douglas to their grandparents' home. Elizabeth always won.

Douglas couldn't understand it. They would start at the same time. Then, Elizabeth would disappear, and he wouldn't see her again until he got to Granny Moore's.

Elizabeth didn't tell him that she had found a shortcut through swampy woods and along rough cattle paths. It was a more dangerous route than the one Douglas took, but it brought her in ahead of him.

In the early 1890s, the weather went "crook." Season after season of floods, monsoons, and winds caused the Kennys' crops to fail and their cattle to die. Mr. and Mrs. Kenny told the children they were going to move away from New South Wales altogether. They were going to Australia's sunny north, to the state of Queensland.

Mr. Kenny made arrangements to ship the furniture. The family packed their bags and boarded the train. Now nearing her thirteenth birthday, Elizabeth gazed glumly out the smoke-smudged window. She was sad and angry about leaving her cousins and grandparents and the high country she loved. She felt as if the best part of her life were ending, and that she had nothing to look forward to.

# Chapter Two

In Queensland, the Kennys first lived on a homestead at Headington Hill. Elizabeth rode a horse to and from school, three miles away.

Country schools went only to the fifth or sixth grade, so Elizabeth's haphazard schooling soon ended altogether. But she still read and read. Sometimes she read aloud to her little brother, Willie, who was frail and couldn't run around and play like other five-year-old children.

Most of the time, though, Elizabeth helped her father with the horses. She knew a lot about horses. An outlaw stallion named Satan wouldn't let anybody but Elizabeth get close to him. She could ride him bareback.

On a pretty spring morning, thirteen-year-old Elizabeth was riding a horse through the fields. She rode for a time at a leisurely pace. Then, remembering the races with her cousin Douglas, she urged the horse to a gallop. A sudden movement beneath her sent her stomach plunging. The saddle was slipping! She tried to slow the horse, but it was too late. The saddle slid down the galloping horse, and Elizabeth tumbled to the ground.

The well-trained horse immediately came to a full stop—with one of his hooves on the hem of Elizabeth's dress. When she tried to lift the hoof, she realized she had broken her right wrist.

With her left hand, she grasped the horse's hoof and lifted until he took a careful step. She managed to tether him to a tree, then started toward home. Someone saw her walking and knew it could mean only one thing. "Liza's been thrown," the call went out. She hadn't cried until then.

"It's so humiliating," she told her mother.

The accident caused great excitement in the Kenny home. For a broken bone, Elizabeth would have to go to a hospital. None of them had ever been to a hospital. Their mother took care of even serious illnesses like diphtheria with home nursing.

Mrs. Kenny wrapped Elizabeth's wrist with padding and made a sling. Mr. Kenny hitched a horse to the buggy. Elizabeth and her parents bounced and swayed over forty miles of rough roads until they reached the nearest hospital, in Toowoomba.

At Toowoomba General Hospital, they saw Dr. Aeneas McDonnell, the house surgeon. Dr. McDonnell had a handlebar mustache and a gruff manner.

After he had put Elizabeth's badly swollen arm in a cast, Dr. McDonnell told her parents that she needed to stay in Toowoomba for a few days. He invited Elizabeth to stay with him and his wife.

During her five-day visit, Elizabeth told Dr. McDonnell about Willie. "He's not strong like the rest of us," she said. "The twins have to carry him piggyback part of the way home from school." Because Willie couldn't defend himself, Elizabeth told Dr. McDonnell, the other boys picked on him.

Dr. McDonnell suggested calisthenics.

Upon her return home, Elizabeth and Willie worked hard on his bodybuilding sessions, but there wasn't much improvement.

The Kennys moved two more times, settling finally in a place called Rocky Mountain. This time Mr. Kenny bought a farm—eighty acres of land, a good house, and a large barn. They had roses and lilacs, and an orchard that provided apples, apricots, and mulberries.

Elizabeth, eighteen, still brooded about Willie's frailness. They had saved their pennies and sent away for a course they saw advertised in a magazine. The great Sandow, the ad said, could turn a skinny, pathetic-looking body into a handsome, strong one. There were before and after pictures to prove it.

Although Willie did everything the great Sandow said he should do, he continued to look like the before picture.

Elizabeth decided to go see Dr. McDonnell. The Kennys now lived closer to Toowoomba, so she hitched a buggy ride into town with neighbors.

This time, Dr. McDonnell taught Elizabeth about muscle structure and lent her an anatomy textbook.

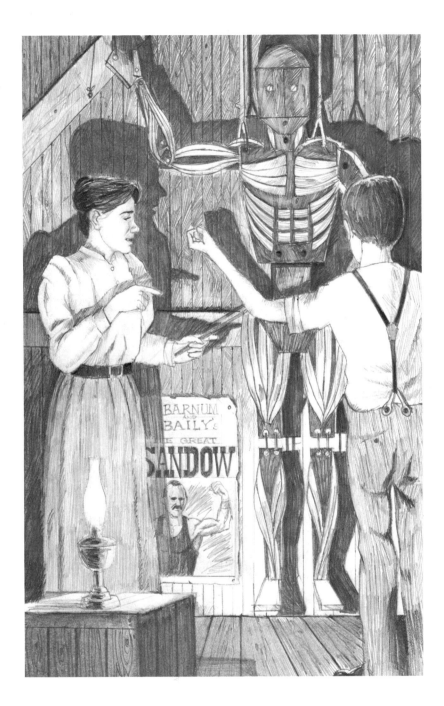

She pored over the book and bombarded Dr. McDonnell with questions.

"When I get home," Elizabeth said, "I'm going to rig up a model to show Willie how his muscles work."

With ribbons, some string, and spare lumber and pulleys she found around the farm, Elizabeth made a wooden model. She explained the muscle structure to Willie so that he could understand how his muscles worked. Once Willie learned how to contract each muscle separately, they developed and grew stronger. Before long, he more than matched the great Sandow's after illustration!

# Chapter Three

As a young woman, Elizabeth had high cheek-bones and a clear, fair complexion. Thick eyelashes set off her brown eyes. She was tall and big boned, and walked with her back straight and her head high. Large, stately women were the vogue in Australia in the early 1900s, but it was considered ladylike for all women to act helpless.

Elizabeth refused to go along with those social rules. "I'm healthy and strong," she said, "and I will not pretend to be otherwise."

Women were also expected to marry. Elizabeth allowed a few young men she met at church or parties to call on her, but she didn't fall in love with any of them.

Still living at home in her mid-twenties, Elizabeth went with her father to Toowoomba to sell their produce. She taught piano and Sunday school. She tried working as a governess, but she found the work confining and boring.

When she was twenty-seven, word came that Grandfather Moore had died. Elizabeth went to Guyra to stay with her grandmother.

Granny Moore, whom Elizabeth resembled, was a handsome woman. She wore a lace collar with a black ribbon around her neck. She looked people in the eye—and she smoked Yankee tobacco in a clay pipe. Elizabeth listened to her reminisce about Grandfather Moore. She visited cousins and old friends in Guyra and out in the country.

They told her they were worried about not being able to sell all of their potatoes. Their usual customers had as many potatoes as they wanted because there had been a bumper crop. Surplus potatoes were rotting in cellars all over the area, they said.

Elizabeth knew there was a shortage of potatoes up north in Queensland. She wired buyers she had met at the Toowoomba produce markets with her father. They wired back that they would be glad to buy all the potatoes they could get.

The New South Wales farmers and their families were grateful to Elizabeth for helping them sell their crops. And she had found a niche for herself as a potato broker.

But her potato brokerage was a venture into a "man's world." That made her unpopular with other young people. Women who had invited her to parties now looked the other way when they met her on the street. "It's disgraceful," they said to one another. "If Elizabeth Kenny wanted to go into business, why didn't she choose something fitting like a millinery shop?"

Elizabeth stayed in Guyra for two years. Then, lonely and unhappy, she decided to return to her parents' home. Looking out the train window at the trees and rivers, she realized she needed a purpose in her life. She wanted to help people somehow. She decided to become a missionary and go to India to serve the poor.

Soon after she arrived at home, she went to Toowoomba to tell her friend Dr. McDonnell about her decision.

"If you're going to become a missionary, you should first learn something about nursing," Dr. McDonnell advised.

That made sense to Elizabeth. She went to Sydney, a coastal city in New South Wales, and worked as a nurse in the slums. Nurses in these poor areas received some training, but they didn't need a degree.

After a year of this work, Elizabeth had earned a vacation. She accepted an invitation to spend a week with a friend who lived in a hilly area outside Guyra.

Elizabeth's vacation had scarcely begun when word came that the wife of one of her hostess's employees was ailing. Although no horses were available and she was not familiar with the area, Elizabeth said, "I'll go."

The employee's house, her friend explained, was three miles away, well out in the bush. She and her daughter walked with Elizabeth to a creek. "You need only follow this creek," her friend told her. "Stay to the left of it, and you'll come to the house."

The sun was low when Elizabeth set out. Light fades quickly in hilly terrain. Dusk, then darkness, closed around her. She still had seen no sign of a house. There was nothing to worry about, she told herself. All she had to do was stay to the left of the creek.

Abruptly, she stopped walking and listened. Water was flowing on both sides of her!

She had missed the house, Elizabeth realized.

She turned around to retrace her steps. But in the darkness she couldn't determine whether she had passed this or that tree or bend of the creek. She didn't even know whether she was going toward, or away from, her destination.

She walked until she was exhausted. There was no sign of a house, nor could she find her way back to her friend's home. Her heart pounded; her stomach tightened.

Sternly, she told herself to relax, that she would find a way out of this. In a blackness softened only by a pale moon, she asked herself what her father would do in a situation like this. She had often heard the stories of his first ten years in Australia. Of how, with everything he owned wrapped in a blanket, he had learned to find his way in strange territory.

Of course! Climb a hill! There was enough of a moon to see water.

Elizabeth climbed to the top of a hill and was able to trace the course of the creek and make out a rooftop. Clinging to tufts of grass and walking sideways to keep from losing her footing, she went down the hill toward the house.

She reached a wire fence that enclosed a garden and orchard, but she couldn't find the gate. She was about to give the Australian call, "coo-ee," which can mean anything from hello to help, when a male voice behind her asked if she needed help. She turned to see a tall, tanned man.

He had also heard about the sick woman, and had come to see if he could help.

When he couldn't locate the gate either, he heaved a post out of the ground, flattened the fence, and accompanied Elizabeth to the house.

During the course of the night, Elizabeth realized that lonely bush dwellers were in desperate need of someone to help when they were sick. She didn't have to go to India to help people.

She also began to fall in love with the man she met that night. When asked about him later in her life, Elizabeth wouldn't tell his real name. She referred to him as "Dan" because he liked the song "Danny Boy."

Soon after that night, she went to work at a semiprofessional cottage hospital in Guyra. She also continued to see Dan. They quarreled about what he called "this nursing nonsense." He wanted to marry Elizabeth. But first, he said, she had to agree to stop working. At that time, few married women worked outside the home.

One day, Dan arrived to take Elizabeth to a special celebration where they would picnic, dance, and watch horse races. They were about to step into his fine carriage when a twelve-year-old boy rode up on a lathered horse. A neighbor's wife, the boy told Elizabeth, was in premature labor.

"Surely someone else could go," Dan said. "We've looked forward to this day for weeks."

"There's no time to find someone else," Elizabeth said.

"Make up your mind now!" Dan said. "If you go, I'll know you choose nursing instead of me."

Her eyes burning with tears, Elizabeth turned to go back into the house. While Dan drove angrily away, she changed into riding clothes.

Late that night, she laid a tiny son in his mother's arms. She knew it would take a long time for her heartache to heal. But, looking at the mother and child, Elizabeth also knew she had chosen the path she was meant to follow.

# Chapter Four

In 1909, Elizabeth decided she had learned all she could at the Guyra clinic. She commissioned a tailor to make a nurse's uniform. Wearing the uniform, she returned to her family's home in Queensland. She told them she was a nurse and began taking care of sick people out in the bush.

It made no difference to bush dwellers that Elizabeth didn't have an official degree or government certificate in nursing. To them she was simply "Nurse Kenny."

To reach her patients, she rode her horse, Thunderbolt, through tall grasses and scrub forest. She guided him across streams. During the winter, she shivered in cold wind and rain. In summer, she tilted her hat forward to shield her face from the blazing sun.

Elizabeth would stay on a case for as long as she was needed. She often slept on a pallet on a dirt floor. If a mother were sick or had a new baby, Elizabeth did the housework and cared for the children. She charged no fees, but she did accept gifts—a chicken, a leg of lamb, handmade goods—though she did not expect them.

One of the people she helped was an Aborigine tribal chief. Ordinarily, white people and Aborigines, native Australians, didn't mix. But when Elizabeth saw the chief hobbling through a village with one of his legs half-gone, she talked to him and convinced him to let her get a wooden peg leg for him.

When the chief went back to his tribe, his people named him Waddy Mundooee, which means "wood foot." To Chief Waddy Mundooee, Elizabeth was "white fella Mary." She didn't know why, and she didn't argue with him.

One day, Elizabeth received a message to come to the McNeils' home, where she had delivered a baby six months earlier. During that visit, she had become especially fond of three-year-old Amy. Elizabeth rode up just at sunset, expecting Amy and the two older children to rush out to meet her. But there was only ominous stillness.

When Amy's father opened the door, Elizabeth knew from the fear in his face that something was terribly wrong.

She stepped into the long, low room with its hard-packed dirt floor, saw Amy, and drew in her breath. Amy was clearly in agony. One knee was drawn up toward her face. The foot pointed downward; the heel pointed outward. Elizabeth tried gently to move the leg into its proper position. Amy screamed with pain.

Baffled by the strange affliction, Elizabeth said, "I'm going to have to get advice from a doctor."

She rode Thunderbolt as fast as she dared to the telegraph office, five miles away, and sent a wire to Dr. McDonnell in Toowoomba. While she waited for the answer, a neighbor of the McNeils rode up. "Please come to my house when you can," he said. Two of his children, he told her, had also "gone lame."

Five hours after Elizabeth had wired him, the telegram came from Dr. McDonnell. "Infantile paralysis," it said. "No known treatment. Do the best you can with the symptoms presenting themselves."

Infantile paralysis was an ancient disease. But there were still few outbreaks, especially in sparsely populated countries like Australia.

As she rode back to the McNeils', Elizabeth whispered a prayer her mother had taught her. "I lift my eyes to the hills from whence my strength cometh. I can of my own strength do nothing."

At the McNeils', Elizabeth sat watching Amy for a few minutes. Spasm, she decided. The sick muscles were in such pain that they were contorting Amy's leg. Heat would relax cramping muscles; it should also relax muscles in spasm.

She first tried heated salt in a sack. Amy cried out the minute Elizabeth put the sack on her leg. *It's too heavy,* Elizabeth thought, *I have to use something lighter.* She made a poultice with linseed meal. It was still too heavy. Amy moaned and tried to move away from it.

Desperate by now, Elizabeth grabbed a blanket made of soft Australian wool. She tore it into strips, put the strips in hot water, then wrung them out and wrapped them around Amy's leg.

Amy stopped crying and went to sleep. After a short time, she awakened and said, "I want them rags that wells my leg."

During the following days, Elizabeth treated the neighbor's two children and three other cases. The minute the pain subsided, she coaxed the children to start using the afflicted limbs.

Not long after the children's recovery, Elizabeth received word to come to a home deep in the bush where a twelve-year-old girl was very sick. By the time she reached the house, night had fallen. The girl's mother opened the door for Elizabeth. In obvious pain, she told Elizabeth she had been thrown from a horse a few days before and had fractured a rib. Her husband, she said, was miles away at a sheep-shearing shed.

A quick look and a few questions suggested to Elizabeth that the girl had appendicitis. With the faint hope that somebody might be traveling a stock road in the area, Elizabeth stepped outside and gave the Australian call, "Coo-ee."

As she listened for an answering call, she heard chanting and the soft clap-clap of hands. It suddenly stopped. Elizabeth hurried back inside and closed the door, trembling. Her call, she realized, had disturbed an Aboriginal corroboree, a religious tribal dance. All her life, she had heard stories about the evil that befell a white person who disturbed a corroboree. She told herself she didn't believe it. Her hair wouldn't fall out. She wouldn't lose all her teeth.

But the fear was still there.

As she stood against the door, something else occurred to her. The patient seemed to have appendicitis—but some of the symptoms she had seen in the infantile paralysis cases were also present. If it were appendicitis and she applied heat, the appendix might rupture. If it were infantile paralysis and she did not apply heat, the girl would soon be in agony.

While Elizabeth was examining the girl more thoroughly, the family dog growled and went to the door. The corroboree! Already on edge, Elizabeth was close to panic when she heard the familiar thump, thump of a peg leg. She let out a relieved sigh. She was not afraid of Waddee Mundooee.

"White fella Mary in trouble?" Chief Waddee Mundooee asked when Elizabeth opened the door.

In the moonlight, she could see that he and the men standing behind him wore only opossum tails tied to strings around their waists. White paint decorated their faces and ribs. Downy feathers were stuck in blood smeared on their bodies.

Quickly, Elizabeth wrote a wire to Dr. McDonnell. She tossed out a red checked tablecloth to cover the man Chief Waddy Mundooee selected as a messenger, and the man rode off to the telegraph office.

Dr. McDonnell's return wire said infantile paralysis frequently affected the abdominal muscles. Nurse Kenny proceeded as before, first with the hot, wet blanket strips, then with exercise.

Months later, when Elizabeth went to visit Dr. McDonnell, the busy surgeon asked about her infantile paralysis patients. "Are they badly crippled?" he asked.

"Why, no," she said. "They're all fine."

He stared at her. "Come with me," he said.

About the same time she had sent the wire to him, he told her, there had been an outbreak of the disease in Toowoomba. Doctors there had followed treatment methods recommended by world experts.

Dr. McDonnell opened the door to a ward. Elizabeth looked with horror at children whose limbs or entire bodies were imprisoned in heavy casts.

# Chapter Five

Nurse Kenny asked Dr. McDonnell why the infantile paralysis patients were being encased in casts and splints. He told her that doctors believed the patients' spasms were caused when healthy muscles pulled limp, infected muscles out of shape. The limbs, left untreated, became deformed and paralyzed. Although the doctors hadn't been able to prevent paralysis, they believed immobilizing the limbs would at least prevent deformity.

With her cases, Elizabeth had applied heat and moisture until the spasm subsided, then she encouraged her patients to exercise.

Her patients had recovered the use of their stricken limbs. And there had been no deformity!

She wanted to let the doctors know what she had discovered. But how could she get them to listen to her? She was not a physician. She wasn't even a real nurse. Maybe, she decided, she could show them. She could open her own semi-professional hospital and treat infantile paralysis patients.

With the money she had saved from her potato business, she bought an old six-room frame house in Clifton, Queensland. It served both as her home and as a hospital. She named her hospital Saint Canice's.

The poor brought their children with injuries or ordinary ailments to Saint Canice's. But if the terrifying disease of infantile paralysis struck their children, most parents still took them to a doctor. Since Elizabeth knew the children would be put in casts, she asked the doctors to send these patients to her. The doctors refused.

Some parents, however, did have faith in Elizabeth and brought their stricken children to her. "They take them home with no disabilities, but the doctors withhold their recognition," a frustrated

Elizabeth wrote home to her mother.

In 1913, Elizabeth's father died and her mother came to live with her. Then, in 1914, Great Britain declared war on Germany. When Australia joined Great Britain in the fight, Willie (now called Bill) immediately volunteered.

Elizabeth knew there was a shortage of military nurses. Her work at Saint Canice's would have to be interrupted. Dr. McDonnell helped her to bypass a military restriction that all nurses must be certified, and she joined the Australian army. Elizabeth sold Saint Canice's and sailed to England. After a short training period, Staff Nurse Kenny was sent to the front.

She served in tents close to the trenches in Belgium and France. She was then transferred to a hospital unit set up in a French convent. Day and night she could hear shells bursting.

Nurse Kenny was at a patient's head and an English nurse was at his feet when a German shell tore into the convent. In a daze, Elizabeth stared at the other nurse and the patient. They were both dead. The other nurse's hand still cupped the soldier's foot. Shell fragments had torn into Elizabeth's knee and the calf of her left leg. She fainted from shock and pain.

When she came to in a convent bed, she looked at herself in a hand mirror. She noticed that her hair, which had been a dark brown only weeks before, was turning gray. She was thirty-five years old.

After her recuperation period, she was assigned to a hospital ship taking wounded soldiers back to Australia. Hospital ships were called "dark ships" because they didn't use lights. At night on the sea, light is visible from far away. Despite their precautions, enemy torpedos sank some dark ships.

While she served on dark ships, Elizabeth became chief nurse. She was commissioned "sister," the Australian military equivalent of first lieutenant. Proud of her commission, she ever afterward preferred to be called Sister Kenny.

By the time World War I ended in 1918, Sister Kenny had served on more dark ships than any other nurse in the world.

Shortly after the war, a deadly influenza epidemic broke out in many countries, including Australia. Sister Kenny worked hard to help the victims—until she herself collapsed.

Three physicians examined her and agreed that she had a serious heart condition and about a year to live. She heard them talking, got out of bed, and dressed. "If I have only a little time left," she said, "I'm not going to spend it in a hospital."

Elizabeth had to walk with two canes, and often fell limp into bed. She again wound up in the hospital. The doctors narrowed her remaining time to four months.

Elizabeth thought about all the things she wanted to do in her life. She had the money from the sale of Saint Canice's. She had her war pension. She had friends and relatives in England, France, and Ireland with whom she could stay. She might as well make the most of her four remaining months.

She went to all three countries. For good measure, she stayed six months instead of four. Upon returning home, she visited Dr. McDonnell. "Well, I'm still here," she said.

Her health improved, and once again her days became full of taking care of others. She met an eight-year-old girl, Mary Stewart, who needed either a foster home or to be adopted. Sister Kenny adopted her. Mary and Elizabeth's mother became fast friends and constant companions.

Townspeople called on Elizabeth for help when

they were sick. Sometimes they needed hospitalization. Even small towns now had ambulances, but roads were rough and hospitals were often many miles away. Patients on ordinary stretchers, pieces of canvas between carrying poles, sometimes went into shock from the jolting ride. Elizabeth decided to design a better stretcher.

Her stretcher had a plywood base and straps to hold the patients steady. Springs, a firm mattress, and rubber-tired wheels kept them from being jolted. She named it the Sylvia Stretcher after a girl whose life the first model probably saved.

Sister Kenny patented her invention and traveled to other countries to sell it. One of those countries was the United States. Until recent years, the Sylvia Stretcher was still used in the rugged hill areas of the Ozark Mountains in Arkansas.

By 1932, when Sister Kenny was fifty-two, infantile paralysis (also named poliomyelitis and commonly referred to as polio) was occurring at an alarming rate. With each outbreak, the number of cases increased. Once again, Sister Kenny joined the fight against this crippling disease.

She opened a backyard clinic in Townsville, a

warm Australian coastal city, to treat people crippled by polio and other diseases. She still believed she could most benefit patients in the early stages of polio, but because the disease was so terrifying, most patients went to their doctors first.

She asked the Australian Health Ministry to recognize the clinic's work so that more polio patient's would be treated with her methods. When it wouldn't, she didn't give up. She tried harder.

Elizabeth studied medical books and anatomy books, but mostly she learned from her experience. She tried some of the techniques of a new field, physical therapy. If they worked, she kept them. If they didn't, she discarded them. She tried methods never used before. She developed a unique therapy and presented a revolutionary concept: *We are the masters, not the servants, of our bodies.*

She was able to get results when no one else could. There were patients who had been on crutches for years who could walk without them when they left the clinic. Word of the "miracles" in the backyard clinic spread.

Finally, doctors with the Australian Health

Ministry became interested in the clinic. They asked Sister Kenny to explain her methods. Elizabeth didn't know their medical language, and when she used her own terms for the things she'd observed, the doctors couldn't understand her.

Her results, however, were impressive enough that she gained some important government support. More Kenny clinics opened. But some medical people in high places opposed the clinics, and a battle began between those for and those against the clinics.

In October of 1935, the state of Queensland established a Royal Commission of eight doctors to investigate Sister Kenny's methods.

In her eagerness to impress the investigating doctors, she sometimes exaggerated her successes. The doctors were quick to point out any false information. Knowing that some of her reports were misleading, many doctors dismissed all of her results.

The battle over the clinics continued, and the Queensland Royal Commission still withheld approval.

Discouraged by the long fight, Sister Kenny went to England. There she was given her own ward at Queen Mary's Hospital for Children in

Carshalton, outside of central London. Her section at Queen Mary's grew from one ward to three.

The British report of Sister Kenny's work was glowing. She felt certain she would now get the support of the Queensland Royal Commission.

She was about to return to Australia when word came that her mother, now ninety-three, was very sick. Elizabeth immediately left on a seaplane. A few weeks after Elizabeth reached home, Mrs. Kenny died.

At the beginning of 1938, a polio epidemic struck Australia, and the Royal Commission issued its long-awaited report on Sister Kenny's work. All 130 pages condemned her. Her abandonment of splinting, it said, "was a grievous error." Her many treatments were "unnecessary."

At first Sister Kenny was so depressed that she couldn't fight back. But that didn't last. She squared her jaw, jutted out her chin, and started swinging.

Some important doctors fought beside her. After seeing the results of her work during the epidemic, they urged the Royal Commission to reconsider.

It wouldn't.

In 1939, Germany invaded Poland. War news

filled the newspapers. Sister Kenny and her work against polio were ignored.

There were far more polio cases in the United States than in Australia, her supporters pointed out. They told her they would finance a trip to the United States for her and her daughter, Mary, now a trained Kenny therapist.

On March 29, 1940, Mary and Sister Kenny, now almost sixty years old, set sail for America.

# Chapter Six

Carrying official letters to the National Foundation for Infantile Paralysis and the Mayo Clinic, Sister Kenny and Mary arrived in San Francisco on April 14, 1940. Word of Sister Kenny's treatment had reached America, and newspapers sent reporters to meet them.

The American public had a great interest in polio, which was striking more and more frequently. Everyone knew President Franklin D. Roosevelt had contracted polio as a young father. Heavy braces encased his legs from hip to toe.

Holding on to her big hat to keep it from flying off, Sister Kenny declared, "I have found the best treatment for infantile paralysis yet devised."

Wherever she went, reporters asked her questions. When asked about her education, she said she had graduated from Saint Ursula's College. She told them she had received her nursing training at Toowoomba General Hospital.

She believed doctors wouldn't listen to her if they knew she was not an educated, certified nurse.

Doctors and nurses were disappointed when they met Sister Kenny. A nurse described her as looking like "a country bumpkin." She spoke in a monotone and didn't use the usual medical terms in describing polio. "She seems to be talking about a different disease," medical people said.

Disappointed that American doctors were not willing to accept her theories, Sister Kenny was ready to go home. Then, Mary reminded her of their letter of introduction to the Mayo Clinic.

When they arrived at the Mayo Clinic in Rochester, Minnesota, the doctors were more receptive and listened closely to the things Sister Kenny said.

There were no polio cases in Rochester, they told her, but there were in the nearby Twin Cities, Saint Paul and Minneapolis. The Mayo Clinic doctors set up appointments for her.

Although they were skeptical, Twin Cities doctors let Sister Kenny *show* them, rather than tell them, what she could do. They were amazed.

Dr. Miland Knapp and Dr. Wallace G. Cole made arrangements for Sister Kenny and Mary to stay and continue their work.

One of the patients Dr. Knapp asked Sister Kenny to see was a boy named Jack Ruff. Jack was still at Saint Barnabas Hospital in Minneapolis eight months after a polio attack. His shoulder and his arm were enclosed in an airplane splint, which caused his arm to stick straight out from his side.

The splinting was the result of the same theory Sister Kenny had been fighting from the time she was a bush nurse. The doctors believed that Jack's affected muscles were flaccid, or limp, like wet rope.

"Flaccid, my eye," Sister Kenny said. "If you take his arm out of that contraption, you'll find his arm so stiff you can't *force* it down to his side."

When the cast was removed, she was proved right.

The doctors began to understand what Sister Kenny had been trying to explain. The "flaccid" muscles they were treating were actually the ones that *had not* been invaded by polio. They couldn't move because when neighboring sick muscles were in spasm, the nervous system shut down and stopped the healthy muscles from working, too. Bound in casts, the nerve paths to healthy muscles stopped working, and the muscles became paralyzed.

Sister Kenny offered to take on Jack's case. That was in early summer. When snow fell in November, Jack was out shoveling. And Mary and Sister Kenny had found a second homeland.

"This time," Sister Kenny told Mary, "I'm going to win. We'll see those hateful splints burned!"

Sister Kenny was assigned a ward at Minneapolis General Hospital. She awoke at 4:30 in the morning and took a taxi to the hospital. She drank a cup of tea, started to work at 5:30, and worked until midnight. She was not a salaried employee, and she did not accept money from patients' families. If someone sent money, she turned it over to the National Foundation for Infantile Paralysis. They, in turn, sent Sister Kenny a small amount of money for living expenses, but it didn't go very far.

Jim Henry, president of the Minneapolis Exchange Club, found out that Mary and Sister Kenny were eating almost nothing but tea and toast. After that, the Exchange Club financed her stay in the United States.

The winter of 1940 in Minnesota was a bad

one. The worst blizzard in fifty years struck on November 11.

"If only it weren't so cold," Sister Kenny often said to Mary. "And they still aren't giving me acute cases to treat. Maybe we should go back home."

On the evening of December 23, Dr. John Pohl was coming to dinner. Sister Kenny had forgotten to buy cream. Walking back from the corner grocery store, still wondering whether she and Mary should go home, she slipped on some ice. As she fell, she instinctively threw out her right arm to try to catch herself. She heard a crack and felt a sharp pain in her wrist. Nobody had to tell her what had happened. She knew. She had been through this before, long ago when she fell from a horse in Queensland.

The building caretaker helped her to her apartment, and Sister Kenny was attempting to straighten her own arm when Dr. Pohl arrived. He immediately ordered her to a hospital.

Sister Kenny had to spend Christmas day in the hospital. Not being able to work made her miserable. "This confinement is unbearable," she told Mary.

A week later, at the beginning of the new year,

she was back at work. And she had decided not to go home. She had realized that she couldn't stand not being able to continue her work with polio victims. In America, she had that opportunity.

# Chapter Seven

At last, in 1941, the doctors at Minneapolis General Hospital asked Sister Kenny to work with acute cases of polio. Almost immediately, news of her dramatic results travelled through the medical community and to the public.

Polio was spreading so rapidly that all people were afraid for themselves and their children. News of Sister Kenny's successful methods gave them hope. The city of Minneapolis bought a house for her, and on December 17, 1942, the Sister Kenny Institute was dedicated in Minneapolis.

Sister Kenny found it necessary to hire a secretary, Margaret Opdahl, who had herself had polio as a child. Margaret knew Sister Kenny was working too hard, but she couldn't make her slow down. In addition to nursing, Sister Kenny gave talks. She also wrote magazine articles and collaborated on books about her work and her life.

In 1943, a bad polio epidemic hit the United States. There were 12,450 cases, almost 3,000 more than in 1940. Once it began to spread, polio was as hard to stop as a forest fire.

Every day Sister Kenny would work, sleep a few hours, and go back to work. She treated patients, taught doctors and nurses, and trained therapists in cities across the country.

Still defensive with doctors, she was like a different person with patients, especially the children. When she walked into a children's ward her face softened and she smiled.

The children were also at ease with her. "Hi, Sister," they would call out.

She joked with them, and they joked with her.

Then they got down to the serious business of working together to get well. Even three-year-olds knew the correct names for their afflicted muscles.

"It's really the patient who must reopen the nerve path to the muscles," Sister Kenny explained.

During the 1943 epidemic, the National Foundation for Infantile Paralysis had a stockpile of splints. It received requests for only three! Sister Kenny was jubilant. Finally, her methods were being accepted wholeheartedly.

She became a heroine to the American people. A movie was made about her life. Sister Kenny went to its premier in New York City on September 27, 1946. Twenty thousand people jammed Times Square to get a glimpse of her.

She enjoyed being famous and the opportunities it gave her. She traveled home to Australia and to England, Canada, South America, France, Belgium, Russia, and many cities in the United States, giving lectures and teaching the Kenny methods.

Margaret Opdahl often traveled with Sister Kenny. Sister Kenny liked for them to get to the train station early. That was one of the few times she could relax. While they waited, they might have Sister Kenny's favorite drink, a "black cow," root beer with ice cream floating in it.

Polio epidemics raged. Each time they struck, they were worse. In 1948, there were 27,726 cases in the United States. In 1949, there were 42,033 cases.

Sister Kenny was even more frequently in the public eye. Universities awarded her with honorary doctorate degrees. There were Kenny clinics in New York, Michigan, California, and Illinois. In 1950, she tied with Eleanor Roosevelt as the most admired woman in America. That same year, Congress passed a bill allowing her a citizen's access to the United States. Only two other people had ever been granted that privilege. They were General Lafayette of France, who fought on America's side during the Revolutionary War, and Sir Winston Churchill, Prime Minister of England during World War II.

Despite the acclaim and the victories, Sister Kenny couldn't rest. Her enemy—polio—still prevailed. She talked constantly about a vaccine. If the researchers would listen to her, she said, they would find one.

During the summer of 1952, the most severe

polio epidemic ever hit the United States. There were 57,879 cases.

In Toowoomba, where Sister Kenny now lived when she was in Australia, she began making plans to return to the United States. Her friends and family knew it wouldn't happen. She was seriously ill with Parkinson's Disease.

The 72-year-old warrior had a stroke on November 24, 1952. She died six days later on November 30.

She had always said she wanted to be buried out in the country under a gum tree. The hearse traveled slowly across country roads from Toowoomba. Farmers stood beside the roads with their hats off. As the funeral procession went through the town of Nobby, the pupils stood in front of the school with their heads bowed.

Just beyond Nobby, the hearse stopped. Sister Kenny was buried between two giant gum trees in a little cemetery flanked by wheat fields.

Less than two years after her death, her dream of a vaccine to prevent polio was realized. Developed by Dr. Jonas Edward Salk, it was widely distributed in 1954.

Today, Sister Kenny is considered the mother of modern physical rehabilitation. Her techniques have helped millions of people. The Sister Kenny Institute serves as a residency for medical students specializing in physical medicine. It constantly strives to find better treatment methods, and shares its findings with the world medical community.

# SOURCES

**Primary Sources:**

Interviews of Sister Kenny's friends, fellow workers, and patients.

Letters to and from Sister Kenny, unpublished. Minnesota Historical Society.

Sister Kenny's handwritten memoirs, unpublished. Minnesota Historical Society.

Kenny, Elizabeth, in collaboration with Martha Ostenso. *And They Shall Walk*. New York:Dodd, Mead & Company, 1943.

Kenny, Sister Elizabeth. *My Battle, My Victory*. London: Robert Hale Limited, 1955 (published posthumously).

Pohl, John F., M.D., in collaboration with Elizabeth Kenny. *The Kenny Concept of Infantile Paralysis and Its Treatment*. Minneapolis:Bruce Publishing Company, 1943.

**Secondary Sources:**

Cohn, Victor. *Sister Kenny, The Woman Who Challenged the Doctors*. Minneapolis:University of Minnesota Press, 1975.

Colbeck, Maurine. *Sister Kenny of the Outback*. Edinburgh: Edinburgh House Press, 1965.

Knocke, Frederick J., M.D. and Lazelle S. Knocke, R.N., *Orthopaedic Nursing*. Philadelphia:F.A. Davis Company, 1954.

Schnittkind, Henry Thomas. *Sister Elizabeth Kenny*, (Lives to Remember Series). New York:Putnam, 1958.

*Sister Kenny*, booklet. Minneapolis:Hennepin County Historical Society, 1978.

*Where Quality is a 100 Year Tradition*, booklet. Minneapolis: Abbott Northwestern Hospital, 1982 (American Rehabilition Foundation, parent company of Sister Kenny Institute, merged with Abbott Northwestern in 1975).

Copy 1

B
KEN

Copy 1

Crofford, Emily

Healing Warrior:A Story About Sister
Elizabeth Kenny

| | DATE DUE | | |
|---|---|---|---|
| 3ST | FEB 04 '93 | | |
| JAN 24 '91 | FEB 11 '93 | | |
| JAN 31 '91 | FEB 25 '93 | | |
| FEB 1 5 '91 | APR 12 '93 | | |
| JAN 10 1992 | APR 26 '93 | | |
| JAN 17 1992 | MAR 0 8 1994 | | |
| JAN 24 1992 | MAR 15 '94 | | |
| JAN 3 1 1992 | | | |
| JAN 21 '93 | | | |
| JAN 28 '93 | | | |
| | | | |